Coffee With Teardrops

Kate Fountaine

For:

My overthinking heart
My broken mind
My healing soul
And
This reader.

"If you don't know where you are going any road can take you there"
— Lewis Carroll

Herstellung und Verlag: BoD – Books on Demand, Norderstedt

ISBN: 978-3-7504-1968-1

content

smile

Birds

Look up to the sky.
With their little wings, they fly.
Wherever they want to.
Whenever they want to.
They are
                    free.
Fly away.
Disappear in the sky
On days like this,
I wish I was a bird.

Do it

Most teenager only care about sex, weed and parties. And yes, it is a part of growing up.
It's a part of experience and finding yourself.
Some are finding their self in working or their passion.
Others do it with traveling.
Anyway, they have all at least one thing in common.
They live.
And that is what I want you to do.
Live your life.
You don't have to try everything out.
But take risks and also their consequences.
Then in the end you have only one life to live.
Take every chance you get and especially:
Smile.
Don't waste your time on being sad.
Don't let your life pass you by.
Just live. Just do it.

You and me

Again, I'm laying in my bed on my cushy
pillow, wrapped up in my cozy blanket like a
burrito and thinking about you.
How lucky I am.
Cause I am just a little sand corn
on a great big beach.
But you choose me.
Even though I was tuff and rough like a
cactus and pushing people away. You still
wanted me.
Only me.
You changed me. In a good way. A way no
one else could.
Made me soft, more sensitive, open up and
most important: you made me happy.
With you I can be a child again.
Silly. Weird. Loud. Real. Just myself.
And I remember that every time I look at you,
think about you or see pictures of us.
You built me a castle
Even if it was only made out of carton.

You made me compliments and gave me all of the love I never felt before.
And there is nothing else I need in my life.
Only you.

Happily, ever after (or just for right now)

Do you know that feeling?
That feeling when you're just, happy.
When everything around you stops to be.
But in the same time, the world spins around you, even faster.
And all you do is enjoying the moment.
Every second of it.
You don't think.
You just feel.
All your problems and worries are gone.
When there are butterflies in your stomach.
When you feel like an innocent little child again.
When you are lost in the moment.
When you think that there is nothing you can't do.
When you feel like you have everything you need in life and don't need anything else.
When everything is just perfect.
That is pure happiness.
-That is, when I'm with him.

Three words story

Today
Here
Now
-they can change your whole state of mind

Inside you

You hurt me.
You keep hurting me, all the time.
And it's fine. It's okay.
I can see the mask you're wearing.
You are in pain and you are scared.
You are broken deep inside.
So, you search for someone you can hurt.
Before you get hurt yourself.
You are better than this.
You could do better than this.
You don't have to do that.
But it's okay.
You can't strike me down, not anymore.
Go on and let it out on me.
I can handle it, somehow.
I hope that someday, you'll be free.
Free from the pain.
And that someday you are happy.
But till then I'll stay strong.
And I will go on.

Your worth

Your skin…
Your hair…
Your shape…
Your size…
Your language…
Your origin…

…does not stop you from being a good
person.
…does not say what you can or can't do.
and
…does not doubt your worth.
-be who you want to be

Sun and moon

We are like day and night.
We can`t meet each other.
We can`t see each other.
We are not meant to be together.
But still we know that
on the other side;
one is thinking about the other.
one is waiting for the other.
And that keeps my faith.
And that keeps my smile.

Even better than before

When it seems like
your world is falling apart,
don't break down, don't cry.
I will be there, and we will build it up again.

Movie

Just like in movies or written in books:
I was sitting in the library and he walked in.
What a cliché, right?
We looked at each other and there was
something.
It felt like I'd known him for a lifetime. And
the way he looked at me showed me that he
felt it too.
Instead of sitting at a table in the middle of
the room, he sat at the table on the very back.
The nearly hidden one at the windows.
My table.
Not a word. Just the two of us.
In a world of our own. And that was it.
That was the moment.
That was the beginning of something new.

Shining star

I'm one of those people who are addicted
to the darkness.
Didn't you ever recognize its beauty?
When it is dark outside everything seems so
different. Like a whole new world.
Scary, mysterious and so magnificent.
When there are no streetlamps and the moon
and stars are shining above you and lighting
the world.
Everything is quiet and calm and seems
asleep.
The flowers and their bees.
The dog which chased the cat.
Only in the cities are still some lights on from
people which are working or going out.
But not me.
I just sit here, enjoying the beauty of the night
life
and wondering
When I am going to be a star.
Shining on the great night sky.

Talks

People are going to talk.
About you.
About what you do.
About what you say.
About what you think.
Whatever you do.
So, mind your own business.
Let them talk.
And keep a smile.

In this moment

How about we stop
being so scared of losing each other
and just be together.

Why not

Breath in. Breath out.
The pain, the anger, the sadness,
Put it all together, in your strength and swim.
Don't think, don't feel just swim.
It's the only thing what keeps me on the
ground.
After an hour my body is done.
Exhausted and tired I'm getting out of the
school swimming pool. I'm getting my water
bottle and down it in one swig.
"Someone had a lot of energy to get rid of
huh?"
I was so shocked that I dropped my bottle.
Green eyes are looking at me. I don't know
that guy. I would've remembered such a
body.
"Shit. Sorry haven't seen you there. Actually,
I've never seen you here before at all. You're
new here?"
"Yeah, kinda."
"Do you always express yourself so specific?"

"Maybe. Was what that about? I've seen fast
swimmers before but not like that."
What does he care? And who the hell is he.
"Like you said. Had a lot of energy."
"How come?"
"You're pretty curious, aren't you?"
"Hmm just interested in what I like. A like
that could upset a pretty girl so much that
she's acting like something is going after
her."
Did he call me pretty? He's really sure of
himself isn't hr. I mean I can see why though.
"You're flirting now?"
"Depends. Does it work?"
"Not really."
"So, I have to try harder?"
"Do you say this to every girl in a pool?"
"No, I'm sorry this is my first time."
I can't hold a smile back. Now he's blushing.
But keeps talking.
"Let's make a deal?"
"A deal?"
"Yes. A race. Swim race."
"What does the winner get?"

"Well, if I win.."

"That won't be the case, but go on."

"Sure. Anyway, if I win you have to go on a date with me."

"Fine. And what do I get?"

"If you win, I have to go on a date with you."

What the hell why didn't he just ask me.

"Okay so either way we're going on a date?"

"Guilty."

Jerk. But why me.

"Why?"

"Why not?"

That is not an answer."

"It is. So, you're in?"

"You don't even know me."

"That's what I'm trying to change."

"Why though?"

"Why not?"

"Idiot."

"It is an honor to be one. Now, what do you say?"

"Well.

Why not."

Reading

There are no bad books
there are only bad readers.
-it's all about understanding sweetie

Right now

Oh love.
You don't have to smile all the time.
No one can be happy every day.
But I want you to keep your smile.
It is so pretty, mesmerizing, magnificent.
Keep on going and don't hold on
on being sad.
Your smile is a story.
It tells your story.

Puzzle

"To be honest it is very easy. It is like
puzzling.
It takes time and effort to put everything
together. And if you try it with violence you
know that something is wrong.
But in the end, everything fits together."

"And so is life."
-you are special, JMP

Show me how to dance

The way you laugh
the way you look
the way you smile
the way you talk
the way you say:
" uhm fuck. no idea ugh"
makes me smile.
Every day and all the time.

tears

Maybe forever

You looked at me.
I saw the fear in your eyes.
You asked me if I will love you forever.
I didn't know why you asked me that.
Your eyes told me that you needed an
answer.
The way you looked at me showed me
you were scared.
But I took your hand and touched
your rosy cheek.
Then I looked deep into your eyes and said:
"Oh honey, I can't tell you that."
You wanted to turn away, but I took
you even closer to me.
"But listen. What I can tell you is that:
The day I will stop loving you,
will be the day I'll close my eyes forever."

To my pillow

Sometimes I feel like a little flower.
Tender. Needy. Gentle. Delicate.
And if touched and treated to roughly,
Then withering and fading.
And yes, I cry a lot.
So a thankful letter to my pillow:
Every time I switched off the light and the
darkness appeared you were there for me.
When I cried over my broken heart and a lost
love.
When I whined because of my indecisive self.
I'm sorry for the times I hit you caused of all
the anger about myself.
And also, for every time I screamed at you to
get rid of my feelings.
Dear pillow
Thank you for all the tears
you wiped away.
-3.42am

Ocean

Every day I drown in you,
sinking so deep
till every inch of my lung
is filled with you.
You are an ocean.
Dark. Cold. Mysterious.
But still so beautiful.

Expiry date

People say: every relationship has an expiry
date.
That the clock is ticking, and time and life
goes on.
That when trust is gone, no chains or
apologies could fix it.
Cause chains are just jewelry.
And apologies only letters formed to words.
Even if I want a forever with you
I may can't have it.
And even if we laugh together now
We may won't do it later.
So, let's just enjoy here and now.
The clock is ticking.
-I already miss you

Used to be

He was the one I opened up to.
He was the one who never made me cry.
He was the one I always wanted to make happy.
He was the one who never judged anyone.
He was the one you could trust to the most.
He was the one who made me feel home.
And…
He was the one who broke me.
Still…
He is the one who's absolutely perfect.
He is the one I just can't let go.
He is the one I have to take care of.
He is the one I don't want to lose.
But…
He is the one who keeps hurting me the most.
After all…
He is the one I truly love.

The pain

Crying so hard that you can't breathe.
Trying to live but going beneath.
Hurts so much that you want it to end.
But day after day you smile and pretend.

Again and again   I

It's my fault.
Again.
I haven't done anything.
Again.
And doing nothing is exactly what I did.
I saw her crying, even though she smiled.
I could've went to her, could've helped her.
But I didn't.
Again.
I have no idea why. Why didn't I?
I could've been there for her.
But I wasn't.
And even worse is, that she knows that too.
I screwed up.
Again.
I don't think, that she will forgive me again.
She hates me for sure.

Again and again   II

I screamed for help.
He said, I have to tell him if I need him.
He said, I have to be clear with him.
Cause otherwise he wouldn't get it
So, I did.
Damn man.
I called you.
I needed you.
I was done.
I was broken.
And I was all alone.
He wasn't there for me.
Again.
He hurt me.
Again.
But I know I'll forgive him, again.
Cause I love him and always will.

She was

She started crying. Every time she looked in
the mirror she started to cry. As if she was
hypnotized from her own reflection. She
couldn't see her own beauty. But believe me
she was. She was so pretty.
Long straight chestnut hair. Tiny freckles
around her nose. And a smile so lovely and
heartwarming.
She had a hard life. You know that? Yeah, a
life of losing her loved ones, diseases and
violence. Tragic. But she never gave up. She
was strong.
Always smiling and trying to make others
happy even if she wasn't happy herself. She
was delighted from everything. A little
ladybug was a gift from heaven to her and a
simple: "how are you", made her day.
She had few but great friends. A wonderful
boyfriend. And she was there for everyone.
Remember that home party you were at? She
went there at 2am. You called her drunk and
in the middle of the night. She went there

picked you up and drove you home. She put
you in your bed, took care of you and stayed
there. She never left your side.
She was there, remember? She always was.
And what did you do for her?
Going to the cinema? Shopping? Getting a
coffee? No. You know what I mean.
Or remember that one night you two went to
that old diner? First you didn't want to, but
she convinced you. Cause she always got
what she set into her mind.
She made you happy. Made you laugh. She
turned on the jukebox and played your
favorite song. Then she danced. In the middle
of the diner.
She didn't care about what others think of her
or that they were staring at her. All she cared
about was you. Always. But you?
You were to blind to see that. You gave up on
her. Left her. Believed her smile and mask.
And now it's too late. Heaven conceived her
with open arms. Took her away and took her
pain. She's gone. You are too late. But at least,
you know, at least she's happy now.

The Night

While he slumbers very deep,
she is crying herself to sleep.

Leaving and left

It hurts.
Really hurts.
You have no idea how much it hurts to leave
you.
I'm hurting myself so badly.
But I rather hurt myself now,
then knowing...
that someday you will hurt me.
And that someday you will leave me.

Because in the end, everyone leaves me
It always is that way.
It has always been that way.
And I tried to think that you are not like the
others.
But then you said some words and did some
things,
which showed me,
that you are, not that different at all.

The difference between you and me

I'm an opportunity.
You are a priority.

Somewhere you can't see me

Stuck...
Trapped...
Caught...

in my mind.
in my thoughts.
in my soul.

Or just gone.

Please, help me to get out there.
Please, help me to be free.
I tried to do it alone, but I know now that I
cant.

Run

"Run. Don't stop. Don't look back. Just run.
Stay where you are alone. When nothing else
is near. Go! Care about yourself. Nothing
else! Now. Leave."
That was what he told me. The last thing
someone said to me the last three days. I ran.
Didn't stop.
Not when I heard them screaming.
Not when they begged for help.
Not when it became dark and cold.
Not when my legs felt like giving up.
I was running. Always moving. Fleeing.
Here I am now. Here where nothing else is
left except of me.
Hidden in a hollow. No food. No water.
Just me. Laying here, heavy breathing.
And knowing that no matter what, I will
survive.
I have to. Someone will find me. Has to.
I won't give up. I'll keep fighting like I
always do.
Always did.

Empty

Being sad all the time is so painful and sucks.
But emptiness and feeling nothing anymore
is hell.
It's uncontrollable and you can't do anything
about it.
You are dark.
Don't feel.
Don't care.
You just exist.

The day will come

When I die
please don't cry
look at the sky
and say "goodbye".

Dead somehow

They say and think that the day you die
is the day you stop breathing.
That's not true.
'Cause the day you die is the day
you stop feeling.

Prove enough

You were scared, you said.
Scared that I would break your heart.
I promised you, I wouldn't.
Because I love you, and that's true.
But still you were scared, and I felt that
you needed proof.
I gave you my love.
I gave you my heart.
I gave you the world.
I gave you the stars.
I gave you everything, you asked for,
everything I had.
Independent of what it takes.
You wanted more. More and more each day.
And then it was enough.
Proof enough for me.
I proved I wouldn't break your heart while
you,
were breaking mine.

Nightmare

There is only one thing worse than a
nightmare.
Waking up and realizing, it's not over.
In your dreams everything is just made up in
your mind. But in life everything is real.
It's where your worst nightmares really come
true.
And that's what scares me the most.
That, if it happens there's no way out.
You can't just wake up.
You are trapped in it.
That is life.

Meet me when you're sorry

I won't.
No, not this time.
I won't call him.
I won't apologize first.
I won't run after him.
Not this time!
Either he cares 'bout me,
or he doesn't.
It all depends on him now.
And that is what scares me the most.
He's important to me.
But am I important to him?

Will he drop me down?
Will I be all alone again?

All the same

We think and see that someone is different
when he talks, looks or acts in a different
way.
But why can't we realize that we all are
different.
We are all the same while we are so different.
It's just that
...some don't want to show it.
...some can't show it.
...some are to afraid, to show it.
That's what society does.

Homesick

I saw you crying.
I went to you and asked if you are okay.
You smiled and nodded but oh darling,
I knew you weren't.
So I asked what's wrong.
"I want to go home.", you said quietly.
I was confused and offered you to drive you
home.
But you shook your head and smiled while a
tear was rolling down your cheek.
"Not that home. My real home."
I didn't know what to say.
So I hugged you and said,
that we all love you here.
For a second we both were quiet.
Then you looked at me, deep in my eyes and
answered me:
"Maybe. Maybe not. But either way,
y'all don't need me here. I have done enough.
I'll show you off.
I'm going back to where we all came from."

Drop

Yes, I cried.
Yes, because of you.
No, I don't love you.
No, I don't hate you.
Maybe 'cause I miss you.
Maybe 'cause you hurt me.
Why can't you understand?
Why don't you get it?
It's simple: you promised.
It's simple: you lied.
This time, it's your fault.
This time, it's your turn.

I won't, run after you.
~~I won't forgive you that, never ever.~~
I will forgive you, always and ever!

But oh silly girl

Why should someone call a fat girl, thin?
Why should someone call a repulsive girl,
cute?
Why should someone call a stupid girl,
smart?
Why should someone call an ugly girl,
pretty?

Why should anyone call you worth it?
-my mirror is talking to me

Little and broken

They don't know our story.
They don't know what we have been
through.
They don't know about our
little
broken
strong
family.

Scary

The world is full of scary things.
Some people are afraid of highs.
Others from darkness.
A few from spiders or snakes.
Then there's me.
I'm not really afraid of anything.
Except of one thing. Myself.
People are afraid of something because they
don't want to get hurt or die.
That is why I am scared of myself.
If anyone or anything would hurt or even kill
me, it wouldn't be my fault.
But if I'd hurt myself... if I'd kill myself
it would be my fault.
Everyone would blame me and in the
meantime their self.
And I don't want that.
So, this is the reason why I am praying every
day for someone or something
that could end my pain except of me.

3am.

I promised that I would stop.
And I did, till now.
I'm not proud of it. Not at all.
But I can't do anything about it.
So here I am. In the middle of the night, or
early morning, at my best friends' house.
In front of his house. Drunk and crying.
I shouldn't do this. I can't and I won't.
I'll turn around and leave. I won't ring the
bell.
I'll just go home.
But now I am already here so why not right?
And without even thinking about it again my
finger touched the doorbell.
Only a second later the door was opened. He.
"What the... damn what are you doing here at
3 am? Damn some people want to.. are you
crying? Why what is..."
"I hate you! You meant everything to me.
You were everything I had. And now you are
gone too?"
"Did you drink again? You promised..."

"No! You promised. Promised not to leave me. You lied!"

"And I didn't. I never left. What are you even talking about?"

"How could you? I needed you, so much. And you went to her."

"What does that have to do with her?"

"Everything! Don't you get it? We were always there for each other. Only the two of us. But now you are gone. And with her."

"Why... why are you telling me this now?"

"Because I love you idiot. I always did. I always will."

"Why didn't you tell me before?"

"'Cause I'm not good enough. I'm no good. No one could ever love me, at all. It doesn't matter how hard I try; I will never be enough..."

"I love you too."

"No. Don't tell me that when you feel guilty. Tell me that, when it is true."

Who to love

But my little girl.
Tell me,
how can you love him so much?
With all your love.
If you don't even know
how to love yourself?

Fri(end)

Usually, something like that wouldn't strike
me down. Because friends stand through
hard times like this, together.
But is that what we are? Friends?
I always thought, friends don't lie.
Friends are there for one another, when they
really need 'em.
Friends support, and don't let each other
down.
Friends trust and defend another, when
haters gonna hate.
Friends do listen and talk
because they want to.
And you did nothing of all this.
So again, is that what we are? Friends?
If not then, what are we?

Wrong

I have to apologize.
Yes, I do.
I just was there for you, so many times.
Tried to make you happy and smile.
Or even just be there for you.
And then I expected the same from you.
That wasn't right.
It is not your job, to make me happy.
To be there for me or support me.
It isn't.
And I forgot that.
I'm sorry for that.
It hurts, a little.
A little quiet much.
But expectations hurt.
They always do.
That's why I gave them up.

They lie

They say, love hurts.
That's a lie.
Love never hurts.
Cause then it wouldn't be love.
The many unfulfilled expectations,
These are which hurt.

Three are one too much

"Come on, I really love you. Please, can't we
just go back to how it was?"
"It will never be how it was before, stop
pretending that to yourself.
You love her.
It always was her, and it always will be her.
I can see the way you look at her.
It's the way, how I always wanted you to
look at me.
It's the way, I always look at you.
And the reason you look at her like that,
the reason I look at you like that,
is because you love her.
And I love you. I love you so much, that
I have to let you go.
Go and fight for her like I did fight for you.
I never loved someone so truly and intense
like   I loved you.
Like I do love you.
And maybe I'll never love someone so much
again.
But I know that I will love again.

Someday.
But for now, I'll let you go.
I'll let you go, and I will never forget you."

xoxo   *your conscience*

He doesn't need you. He doesn't.
He has her.
Yeah you warned him, that she's a liar.
And she hurt many people, inclusive you.
But he does what he wants.
And since he has her, he doesn't need you
anymore.
She makes him laugh, she makes him smile.
That used to be you.
But you mess everything up.
You make him sad and make him mad.
Well if you even talk to each other.
Cause that is what you two stopped too.
You are sorry. But for yourself.
Because while he doesn't need you anymore,
You know you still need him here.
Even though he keeps hurting you.
But as long as he's happy now, happy with
her,
You have to be happy too.
Happy for him.

It will get better

I just want to run away,
it`s like I'm dying here.
Still crying every night and day,
controlled of my own fear.

After life

"Why are you crying?", the boy asked.
"I'm scared", the little girl gambled.
"Scared of what?", he kept asking.
"I'm scared of dying. What comes after life?"
The boy looked at the girl and had no idea
what to tell her. But then he answered:
"Oh, little girl. Dry your tears. A young sweet
kid like you shouldn't think about that. No
one should. Cause death is something we
can't change. You will die. Maybe already
tomorrow. Maybe in 78 years.
We don't know what comes after life and that
can be scary. But it does not have to be.
You can imagine whatever you want. Maybe
you will go to heaven. Maybe you will have a
next life. Maybe you'll go to a world were
fairies exist.
When you are afraid of death then you are
scaring yourself.
Now my lil girl, take your imagination and
create your 'after life'."

love

Hands

I love your hands.
They touched me so softly.
As if I was something that would break down
if it was handled to roughly.
As if I was something so precious you are
scared to hurt if you won't beware it.
Your fingers were sliding down my body.
So smoothly.
So diffident.
So passionate.
Everywhere.
I wanted it to be never ending.
I wanted you forever.

You're my dream

The sun shines and warms our bodies.
We lay on a meadow in a park.
It's wonderful.
I want to remember this moment forever.
I don't want this moment to stop.
I missed this. I missed you.
I put my head on your breast and feel you
breathing.
Breathing in and out. Slowly and calm.
I close my eyes.
Just for a moment.
Being happy and enjoying this.
But when I opened them again, it was gone.
All gone.
It was just a dream.
Made up in my mind. It wasn't real.
But there's something real about it, and that
is you.
And that you are my dream.

Between telling and showing

You can tell someone a thousand times that
you like them or even love them.
they can never truly believe it
till you also show it.

Just friends

He's picking me up at 7pm. Five more minutes.

"Where are you two going?"

"Cinema. A new horror film just came out."

"Aren't you a lil overdressed for that?"

She's right, kinda. I'm wearing my new black jeans and a white blouse with my favorite heels. But for my mum, even a tracksuit is overdressed.

"Nope. It's called style mum."

"If you say so. I guess he's here. Say hey from me."

I hear a car parking in front of our building. We're living in a tiny apartment. Tiny but comfortable.

I'm taking the stairs and I'm faster than it should be possible for me in these shoes. He's waiting in his car. As always.

"Hey there."

"Hey good looking. Aren't you a lil overdressed for a killer clown?"

"Not at all. Always look good for a man who wants to kill you!"
"So, I have to become a murder now?"
We are always like that. Messing around with each other. I pick the music for the drive to the cinema. We have a different taste of music. But there are some bands we both like. As different as we are, we have many things in common. As example the fact that we both hate horror movies. I´m like the scariest person on earth and so is he.
We get a huge bucket with popcorn and take our seats. The movie starts and the lights turn off. I place my head on his shoulder and look at the screen in front of us.
Half of the movie is over and it wasn´t really scary till now. Not even for me. But I know that something is about to happen. I know it. I feel it.
A woman is walking towards a closet. Don´t open it. You know he´s in there. Don´t. She´s getting closer to the closet. Her hand is touching the doorknob. She opens the door and…

"Buuh, he isn't even in there what the…"
Zack. A knife was pulled straight through her
head. I screamed and are so frightened that I
throw the popcorn in the air and it lands all
over our heads.
"Shit."
He laughs. Loud and real. And so cute.
I start to laugh too. But to loud.
A man with a flashlight is walking down the
stairs.
We run out of the cinema as fast as we can.
People stare at us, but we don't care.
But I forgot that running in those shoes may
isn't the best idea. And a second later my face
hit the cold, dirty ground.
"Damn are you okay? Are you hurt?"
"No, I'm fine, I guess. But my shoe isn't."
The heel broke. Great my favorite pair of
shoes is now a piece of trash.
"C'mon. I'll carry you to the bench over
there."
"No, it's fine I can…" But before I could even
finish my sentence, he lifts me up as if I don't
weigh more than a feather.

"Stop let me down, let me down."

He ignores me and won't let me down until we reached the bench. He slowly set me down.

"You are an idiot."

"I know. But a cute one."

"You think so."

"I know so."

He says that with a mischievous smile. I love that smile. It warms my body in a way nothing else does. With him everything is so different.

He looks at me. My face. My eyes. My lips. As if he would see me for the very first time.

"What do you want to do now?"

"There is only one thing I want to do right now."

His eyes get darker. And his voice is quiet. Soft. But still determined.

"And that is?"

He looks at me. Intense. As if there is something he is searching for. He gets closer to me.

"This..."

Kiss. He kissed me. An innocent light kiss.
I was so surprised that I couldn't move for a second.
"But I thought we are just friends?"
"We are friends. Friends who like to do this…"
~a kiss I would wait for forever

Love travels

Wherever.
Whenever.
And whatever will come.
In all the cities, all the states,
in every country, each continent.
On this planet and every other
We will love us, one another.

-always and ever, yours

Home

I'm sorry.
It is as hard for me as it is for you,
I guess.
You give me that feeling I just can't describe.
When we met. When we talked. When we
laughed. When we cried.
That feeling I have with you is just...
I just feel happy. Just for a moment, at least.
When we're all alone, then the feeling is
there.

I know it's been a while since we talked. And
maybe you don't even remember it. But I do.
I remember all our talks and that one feeling.
I remember it pretty well, it is there. I know it
because I feel it every time, I look at you.
When I'm with you I feel save and accepted.
With you I finally,
                    feel home.

Lovely rose

Don't sting yourself on the thorns of the rose
only because she's so lovely.
She will hurt you and you will bleed.
There are other flowers
such as beautiful as the rose is.
-But I don't care about the other flowers.
I only love the rose.
For me she is perfect.
If I have to feel the pain of her thorns
and if I will get hurt
only because I want to touch her
then so it will be.
`Cause for me she is worth it.
-you're my rose

Twinkle   I

I told the stars about you.
Your perfection.
Your mistakes.
Your real self.

Twinkle   II

Look at the stars in the clear night sky.
Then remember.
You
Are
Not
Alone!

Decide

It's confusing. He doesn't know what he
wants. But he can't have everything.
First he tells me that he loves me.
Than he turns away and ignores me.
Just to come back later and to tell me
That he misses me.
I don't know what to do.
I'm confused, sad, then mad and in the end
I just don't care.
And that was when he lost me.
When I stopped caring.
Usually I'm a patiently person but not in this
case.
If he truly loves me, he wouldn't act like that.
When you really, genuinely love someone
then there is no uncertainty, you would never
want to hurt that person.
If you love someone you know it.
-if you love me, let me know

Together

I don't know what the future brings.
Nobody knows.
But I know, that I want you in it.
Maybe we will fight, scream, argue and cry.
But we will do it together.
After all we will reconcile, hug and smile.
And we will do it together.
It absolutely won't be easy.
But that's why it is called
Friendship.
We will live through it, okay?
And it needs both of us.
You and me.
We have to work on it.
Day after day.
I know we can do this, work this out.
Wanna know why I know?
'Cause we will do it,
together.

Tea

You treated me as if my life was a cup of tea.
First you sweetened it,
then you spilled it.

Between the lies

If you only told me lies before,
then I'm not sure,
if I want to hear the truth now.

To my princess

Listen to me. What I'm going to tell you
know is what you have to remember your
whole life.
Promise? So, listen.
I know I barely show it and I don't behave
like others do or I'm going too hard on you...
let's say
I show it in a different way. But I love you.
My beloved, there is nothing on this whole
wide world I could ever love as much as I
love you. You are a gift.
A wonderful gift that was given to me.
And I am so thankful for that. Every time I
look at you and hold you in my arms, I
realize how lucky I am. Without you my life
wouldn't have been fulfilled.
We had our fights and arguments but who
doesn't? You are exactly what everyone calls
perfection.
If anyone else ever says differently and that
you're not good enough or not worth it, than
remember my words.

'Cause you are a dream come true.
And you are loved. Understood?
Even if there's no one near and you feel left alone, you never are.
I am still there and always will be. In your memories and your heart. My love to you will last forever and even longer.
So never doubt yourself.
I know that you can do whatever you set your mind to.
It is in your blood and you will change the world.
My little girl
I am so proud of you
And I love you.

-the love of a father

Sunset

Seeing you leaving me,
is like watching a sunset.
As long as the sun is there
everything's so mesmerizing and beautiful.
Though as soon as the sun has reached the
horizon
the warmth, the light and the love
are gone and the darkness appears.
But with the darkness comes the stars.
And they are there to keep your faith.
The faith that in the morning
the sun will rise again.
And I hope that also you will rise again.
Rise right back to me.

Deserve

You deserve
a person
who says:
I love
your scars
and bruises
as much
as I
love you.

So overwhelming

They asked me how I can possibly be so
obsessed with someone who does nothing
Except of hurting me.
I answered the question with only one word:
Love.
Nothing is as overwhelming and controlling
as love.

Love has many definitions

Love is a great universe with stars and
planets you have to explore, and where you
get lost in.

Love is a vision that is made up in our own
minds and controls us.

Love is nonsense. It's just a fiction made out
of cupidity and greediness.

Love is the meaning of life, the reason why
we even exist and why we are here.

Love is passion and something you're
trapped in.
Love is poison and what hurts you the most.

But I say love is experience.
It is doing, feeling, fighting, crying,
laughing…
Love is everything.
Love is, what you make out of it!

I like games

Compare it with the matching and memory games:
Some find each other earlier, others later.
But in spite of everything, everyone has his partner that belongs to him. Be patient.
That is how love works.

Knowing you

I've seen you laugh.
I've seen you angry.
I've seen you drunk.
I've seen you sleeping.
I've seen your scars
I've seen you naked.
But above all,
I've seen you cry.
So, my love, don't hide from me.
Don't turn away.
Because I know you with all your rough
edges.
And I'm still here.
I'll stay with you.
I'll always love you.

thoughts

Oh, darling

That doesn't help.
Don't cry, dry your tears.
You fell because she pushed you.
But why are you still laying on the ground?
Come on I offer you my hand and
I'll help you to stand up again.
But you have to walk on your own.
And you know that.
You know that life goes on and you know,
that you should too.
Slow down when you're tired,
but never stop going.
'Cause it is so hard to begin again.
You started it, you started to live,
maybe it wasn't really your choice,
but here you are.
So, go on with the story of your life.
Read every page of it, don't skip one,
and don't close the book until you are
at the very end of it.

What life is

It's the end of the beginning.
It's the beginning of the end.
And everything that's in between
is what you have to figure out.

Feelings

Anger	scream
Sadness	cry
Happiness	laugh
Fear	shaking
Drowsiness	sleep
Hunger	eat

To all our feelings there is a reaction.
We cannot control neither of it.
So never blame someone for his feelings or
reactions to them.
Never be ashamed of showing them.
Never.

Little things

You know, life is made out of many, little
things.
And we don't need more.
Eating dinner together at the table.
Watching Netflix together.
Stargazing and cuddling under a warm
blanket together.
Going to sleep and waking up together.
Making each other little compliments.
Listening to another's problems.
It's so less and means so much.
We always think we need to change the
whole world.
But it is more then enough to change
someone's sad face into a smile.
Don't spend your money on something.
Just spend your time with someone.
Then even the highest tree was once a small
seed.

Never ever

Never say never
     and
never say ever.

Because never means never ever,
at no time in the past or future.

And ever means forever,
at any time, all the time and always.

Don't say anything you might will regret,
someday.
You can hurt someone so deeply with words.
And also make someone so happy with them.
Just choose wisely.
Just choose right.

Changes

And when the world is all against you
it is time to make a change.
Both sided.

Memories

This "you still remember..." where you feel
joy, sadness and anger at the same time.

Joy. When someone says
"Do you still know how…"
when you think back to the time and the
things that have given you pleasure.
The time in which you were happy.

Sadness. Because the
"Do you remember where…"
belongs to the past and never comes back.
The happy times you had, are gone forever.

Anger. 'Cause you know that you cannot
help it. There is nothing you can do against
the fact that the past is the past and you don't
get the happy moments back.

But remember, even if the moments, and
sometimes also people, are gone,
the memory lasts forever.

And that is something, no one can ever take away from you.
You just have to keep it in your heart.

-remember me when I'm gone

Strong

To stay quiet and suffer all alone.
To hide the sorrows and the pain.
To cry only when your all alone.

That is so hard. It destroys you and keeps
you strong in the same time.

But oh dear,
To stand up and cry
To say you are not okay
To open up and show your sadness

That is a strength you can be proud of.
'Cause it's not easy.
It's hard and tough.
And it is strong honey.
And in anyway:
You are strong.

Left is the right decision

You only want, what's best for him.
I know that.
You never want to hurt him or do something
that would make him sad.
That's why you let him go, right?
And I'm so proud of you. Really!
 But could you please also do it for yourself?
'Cause it's also the best for you honey.
Well maybe it isn't forever, you know.
You let him go because you love him.
And if he loves you, he'll come back.
And if he doesn't then he's not worth it.
Then it is how it's supposed to be.
So be sad and angry, and then go on.
Be proud of yourself.
Because we are!

Give and get

Give your body
time to heal.
Give your soul
time to clean.

What tears are for

Crying. When tears are running down your
face.
It means so much more.
It is screaming without any noise.
It is begging for help without saying a word.
As you start to cry it means you can't hold
your sadness back any longer.
You are not able to hide it anymore.
And when that happens then scream for help.
Cry it out, beg for help and don't try to do it
alone.
Otherwise it only gets worse.
-trust me

Not someone else's

In our lives we have to confront with many
things.
Many very hard things.
But there is one which is harder than
anything else.
Decisions.
We have to do them all the time, again and
again.
Life is made out of your choices.
Every second we have to make them.
Are you taking a next breath?
Do you stand up?
Will you text that person?
Don't blame anyone else for bad things which
happen, my dear.
Because it is your life,
not someone else's.
And it is made out of your decisions,
not someone else's.

To them

To all the mistreated boys.
To the ones, who were laughed at by mean
girls. Those who felt like there was no one
who could ever love them back.
The `never enoughs` which tried so hard.
To that one who tried to fit in so much.
To all of you, you are worth it.
You are fighters.
It is good to cry.
Don't be afraid to ask for help.
And especially
Don't feel locked out.
Don't degrade yourself.
Never!
-they're telling you lies

Ups

I told my therapist about you.
He was right.
I should've listened to him.

Why care about that

"Things were better when we were kids".
Why so?
Cause when we were younger, we didn't
care.
It didn't matter what clothes you wore, how
you looked or talked. There was good and
bad, and it was so easy to understand.
There were no kissing lips or gender
segregation.
Everything was possible in those days and
that because kids don't care about such little
things.
Why do we? Why does it matter what I wear?
How much I weight.
How my hair looks like.
If I hang around girls or boys.
How big my booty or how thin my waist is.
Why do wall care about such things?
And if I have to make sure of all that, every
day,
only because society does,
then how am I supposed to ever love myself?

Silence

Quiet.
Everything around me stops.
My world stops. And in the meantime,
everything moves. Everything goes on. Life
goes on.
Life never stops to be.
Trees. Leaves. Grass. Roots. Rivulets.
Have you ever recognized the beauty of a
forest?
Ants working. Birds singing. Squirrels
clambering.
And then there's me. Sitting on the mossy
ground and putting my legs into the cold
water of the purling stream. Doing nothing
else then thinking,
About life and freedom. The sweetened taste
of freedom. You never really know what
freedom is till you get it. It's not only going
wherever you want to whenever you want to.
It's more than that.
It's a feeling you can't put into words.

A feeling like, believing you can fly to the moon.
Swim through the deepest parts of the oceans.
Climb the highest mountain of all.
Doing whatever you put your mind to.
It feels like there is nothing that could stop you. And all you need is yourself. That you are free with yourself. What also means that you must be your own best friend.
And that can be hard sometimes. Damn hard. But not impossible.
If that is the price, I have to pay then I will be my own best friend.
I just want … no.
I just need to be free.
Absolutely free.
I mean I am free, right now. Here in the silence. All alone and yet still not alone. But that freedom ends as soon as I leave. It will leave. And I need that freedom to stay no matter where I am.
Actually, I just need something that stays. Just once in my life.

One thing that won't leave.
Something… Someone who comes into my
life and says
"I want to stay. To whatever may come."

F c k

Wisdom:

If life fucks you…
Fuck it back even harder.

You're welcome.

Letting

You care.
Maybe you care a little too much.
Too much about others.
And way too less about yourself.
You are such a lovely person,
but you are also hurting yourself.
You know that holding on
has become so much harder,
than just letting go.
You can't wait for the people to decide
if they want to stay or leave for good.
I say it, as if it is the simplest thing in the
world.
And I know it's not.
But...
maybe, you just have to let go.

How to fix it

The best apology
and only true way
to show that you're sorry
is changed behavior.

An apology without a change
is a lie.

Story

Your life is yours.
My life is mine.
Your story is yours.
My story is mine.
Everyone has his story.
There is so much to tell from our stories.
And in every story there are good like bad
parts.
We can't really decide, how many good or
bad parts our story has.
But what we can decide is,
how we tell the story.

Just a game

Life is like a game.
It begins and ends every day new.
And even though the cards and the rules are
the same, the game is always different.
And yeah, sometimes you lose.
But with time and by learning you will know
how to play the game. And you will win.
And don't forget:
It always starts over.
It always begins again.

Easy

A friend once said to me:

"Why don't we make it, just the easy way?
Otherwise it is totally complicated."

And you know what?
He is right.
Don't make your life even more complicated,
than it already is.

Loving and letting

You become sad when you lose something or
someone you love.
That's natural. That's okay.
But when it's lost, it is gone,
That means you have to let it go.
Otherwise you continue being sad.
And darling,
letting go does not mean stop loving.
It actually means to love even more.
Because love sometimes means to let go.
So, when you lose something, try to be
happy.
It is less painful when you realize that this
person will be happy too.
Let go but keep the memories.
Keep the love.
-I let you go and keep on loving you

It needs so less

The tiniest, tiny light can break the darkness.
But there has to be a light.
Without that light the darkness is all around
you and wont go away. Your eyes will get
used to the darkness, a lil bit at least.
But you will never be able to see through the
darkness and it will never disappear.
Search for that one thing that makes you
smile, even just a little bit. Otherwise you will
never break through the sadness around you.
Search for your light.

Every end can be a new beginning

Here we are, this is the end.
I hope that this end will also be a new
beginning.
You read it. Every page of it.
I asked you not to read it.
I knew it would maybe upset you, confuse
you.
Humiliate you.
Disappoint you.
Or whatever else.
But to be honest, I wanted you to read it, to
feel it.
And this is the end of it.
Is it also the end of us? Are we even still an
"us"?
I always was scared you would find out.
I was scared that you would leave me, hate
me.
Although it is not my fault.
It is how it is.
I'm in love with you.
The moment I first saw you…

The moment we first talked…
I knew I can't ever, let this person go. And I
didn't.
We did fight. We did argue.
But after all, we stayed, somehow.
And that is why, I fell in love with you.
It wasn't something especially you said or
did.
And I can't exactly remember when.
But it happened because of all the little things
you did and said that one day, you smiled at
me and
I realized…
I love him. And don't ever want to lose him.
You are, or maybe were, my best friend.
Even if I wasn't yours. But that's life.
And I'll hope that this isn't the end of our
story.
Yeah, we had our bad chapters but also good
ones.
Come on let's write a new story.
With new chapters.
Let's try to write them as beautiful as
possible.

We'll write every good and bad thing down.
But the most important thing is
that we'll write it together
Please, let's write it together.

With love   your something else

For you

Dear reader.
You finished my book. You read it.
I want to thank you for taking your time.
You read a book that I wrote. This book is a
part of my life. So are you now.
Remember that you are pretty, amazing,
smart, wonderful and so unique.
You are someone no one else could ever be.
Be proud of that.
I am.
I don't have to know your whole story to
know that you are special. Cause everyone is.
And I want you to look into the mirror and
say that to yourself.
Learn to be your own best friend and to love
yourself.
Also, do never let anyone tell you that you
aren't worth it.
Because, you are.
Thank you and smile.

About me

I don't shine brighter than the other stars on
the great night sky.
I'm not a special snowflake falling to the
earth in a heavy snowstorm.
I'm not that one fish you're searching for in
an ocean filled with many others.
I am me. What that means is what I must find
out myself first. But this is a part of me. My
Book.
My thoughts. My soul. My heart.
And everything in between.
Everyone says: Don't judge a book by its
cover.
Well, do it. But if you regret it later,
remember that it is your own fault.
So, this is the work of a 15-year-old lil girl. I
went through a lot and yet I'm not done.

About the book

It's no love story. And still it is.
Cause life is full of love. Everything has to do with love.
My heart and soul are in this book.
My feelings and thoughts are written down here.
Read it and feel it. One by one. Think about it but don't overthink it.
Thanks to all the support of my loved ones.
Even though they don't know that they helped me.
This is not just a book. It's a secret.
And hopefully not the last.